BLACK BOYS DREAMING

Virtual
Verse
&
Pandemic
Prose

**BY KHALIL BARNES, CHASE COOPER,
KEVIN CRAWFORD, & JOSIAH OUABO**

ILLUSTRATED BY TONY WHITE

Illustrations by Tony White

Design by Gigi Mascarenas

Shout Mouse Press is a nonprofit writing and publishing
program dedicated to amplifying underheard voices. Learn
more and see our full catalog at www.shoutmousepress.org

Shout Mouse Press,
1638 R Street NW, Suite 218, Washington, DC 20009

Trade distribution: Ingram Book Group

For information about special discounts and bulk purchases,
please contact Shout Mouse Press sales at 240-772-1545 or
orders@shoutmousepress.org.

To the Black Boys Dreaming

To Mr. Roy from Beacon

To the ballers, bionic babes,
and dragon-slaying
chieftains

TABLE OF CONTENTS

INTRODUCTION
BY THE STORY COACHES

Alexa:

Inspired by Jacqueline Woodson's stunning collection *brown girl dreaming*, the vision of *Black Boys Dreaming* was to continue discussion around Black youth and the power of imagination. In the winter of 2020, Shout Mouse Press and we three Story Coaches took this goal and gathered eight middle school boys from Beacon House who were interested in publishing a book. We asked them, *What is a story that YOU believe the world needs to read?* and watched their pens begin to fly.

At Shout Mouse Press, we support books that center young people from historically oppressed backgrounds, understanding that all young people are experts in their own experiences. Therefore, we knew that when we invited these boys to write the kind of stories that haven't yet been written about Black kids, outside of what we call the "single narrative," they would create worlds in which *anything* they dream of is possible. When there is imagination without the rules of being 'too young' or 'not looking the part,' young people can decide who they want to be, and what kind of world they want to live in.

But even with all these plans for the creation of *Black Boys Dreaming*, there was no way to prepare for the kind of nightmare 2020 would be, nor predict the ways in which not just imagination, but health, education, and the lives of Black youth would be further changed.

Drew:

Indeed! The world blew up.

Okay, sorry, that's hyperbole. Which is a poetic device—the sort of thing we discussed with our young charges. It's sort of hard to turn it off when we're writing about our experiences working with them. But allow me to contextualize. When I say that the world blew up, what I really mean is that by mid-March of 2020, the COVID-19 pandemic had changed the entire way in which we interact. The nation's capital largely shifted to masked up, sanitized down, and shut in. News programs took to projecting omnipresent, stark statistics of infections and deaths. School and work became virtual, restaurants became carryouts, and life became a constant grappling with an invisible plague as many of us were introduced to questions which we never previously had to ask, like: *Where can I find some toilet paper?* and *Am I touching my face way too much, or am I just doing way too much noticing how often I touch my face?* And, of course, *Will things ever go back to normal?*

And so, obviously, no longer able to meet in person, we struggled to adapt. Shout Mouse lent the boys laptops as needed and each Story Coach took on two or three writers, coordinating weekly schedules to meet with each writer one-on-one. Gradually, eight writers ultimately whittled down to four as schedules got shifted, priorities got repositioned, and life got real.

Then, as we moved into the summer, the infamous viral video of Derek Chauvin kneeling on the neck of George Floyd for 9 minutes and 29 seconds reopened ever-fresh, never-healed wounds of racial oppression and police brutality. This sparked international protests, often met by the same sort of vicious state-sanctioned violence being protested in the first place.

All of these historic happenings quite naturally fed into our monthly all-group Zoom sessions with our Black boys as we learned more about where they stood not only with poetry and prose, but with politics and principles. We supported each other as a creative family, checking in on each other not solely as "pensmiths," but as people.

We got into a groove. We guided the boys as they slowly developed their wonderful worlds of basketballers, bowmen, and bionic body parts. We watched the boys grow with their characters as they molded their motives and crafted their quotes. Our Black boys kept working. Our Black boys kept writing. Our Black boys kept...dreaming.

Bomani:

They say that one of the positive side effects of reading fiction is learning to empathize. But *writing* fiction teaches us even more, arming artists with the potent ability to understand the lives of others. The team at Shout Mouse has witnessed this as one of the many skills these young men have learned while walking this strange path with us.

We are releasing this project in a time when the need for acceptance and understanding is more important than ever, a time when articulating your story, and the stories of others, is a much-needed skill. We release this book into a society where Black manhood is being reimagined and reinforced, but in too many cases re-institutionalized, a world where the skills we've practiced—brainstorming ideas, working through tedious drafts, and fearlessly publishing our words—will come in handy.

These Black boys' dreams were given an opportunity to evolve and expand while the world was going haywire around them. These writers gave us a sense of normalcy, a new generation's perspective, and an abundant amount of hope. We are proud of the writers they've become, and the small part we have played in coaxing that writer out of them. We anxiously await the next story they tell, the next dream to come to life on their page, and the amazing futures they dream into reality.

THE TALE OF TWO KOBES

BY KEVIN CRAWFORD

ALLOW ME TO INTRODUCE MYSELF

Hi, my name is Kobe Young
and I am 15 years old.
I live in LA where
people throw parties all night
parties as loud as bombs
so I never get enough sleep.

I need sleep
so I can prepare
for tryouts tomorrow.
When I'm tired, I play like
a sloth trying to climb a tree.

Usually, I play like a superstar
fast and strong,
do the behind-the-back hesitation.
Break ankles and
stare at my opponent
as I hit the 3.

Yesterday, I saw
my friend BJ at the neighborhood
courts. He challenged me
to a one-v-one.

BJ goes to a different school
Jasper High
and plays small forward
for their team.
BJ is like a lion.
He's big, has long hair,
and is the king of the court.

I got blocked by BJ so then I was on defense.
BJ scored on me and then I was on offense,
I snatched BJ's ankles and scored.
I won.
BJ shook my hand
I got skill and a high basketball IQ.
Sure, you're good, but I'm still better

He's right that I'm good.
He's wrong that he's better.

I've thought about what BJ's said over
and over again ever since.
And again, I can't sleep
I go downstairs
and get warm milk,
practice in my head
before I go back to bed.

A DAY IN THE LIFE

I wake up the next day and feel
rested and energetic.
Get my shorts and shoes. Kyrie 6's.

I grab toast and run out of the house to school.
I go to class.
English,
Algebra,
Biology,
Geography,
then Computer Science.
I mostly daydream
I have my hand on my face
pencil in my hand staring off into space.
My eyes are hypnotized—
Why, you ask? Because
I mostly think about basketball.
Yeah, I get B's and C's, I'm an average student
I'm not average, though.

At the end of the day, I let out a sigh and go
to practice.
The coach makes me run the same play over
and over
again.
If I mess up I have to run around the gym
'til practice is over.
It's a long day, but I'm not tired;
I'm motivated to be the GOAT
Greatest
Of
All
Time

After practice,
Coach hands us the schedule
and tells us that we have
a game coming up.
I see that I'm playing my friend BJ.

They start talking about who
I am guarding and it's him.
Coach says, *Don't worry,*
you play like an NBA player
like you belong on the Lakers.

If I played on the Lakers
my mother would be so excited
she'd bounce off of the roof
which is typical because
she shows a lot of emotions.
When she gets angry her freckled face
turns into a puffer fish.
When she gets surprised
she breathes heavily
as if she might faint.
And when she is happy, she smiles
as if her mouth is full of fireflies
buzzing and beautiful.
I am so close with my mother
she's watched me ever since i was born—
watched me do homework
or when I went to the park to play basketball
watched me watch a lot of old tapes on Kobe.
My mom is very supportive.
She always comes to my basketball games.
I am close to my mom
because she likes basketball,
but she loves me.

HOW I GOT MY NAME

I am named Kobe because my mother
used to go to Lakers games
when she was younger.
She was always a big fan
of the Lakers because they
were champions.
For 10 years in a row
she'd sit in row number 3
watching overjoyed
eyes squinting, cheeks lifted
smiling so you can see
all of her teeth.

When she was pregnant with me,
she went to a game to watch Kobe
play against the Utah Jazz.
During the game, Kobe
got the ball
called a play, he shook
his defender making him do a U-turn,
made him stumble, hit the ground.
Then he shot a 3 pointer
and made it.
She not only realized that he
was a superstar, but that he
was passionate.
He was supportive
dedicated.
She wanted me to be
just like him
but better.

At the end of the game

she sat close to where the players were coming out.
She was excited to be around the players.
They were sweaty and stinky
evidence of their hard work.
They have strong arms, they walk tall.
She saw Kobe
waved at him aggressively with two hands.

"Kobe! Over here! Hey! Hey!" she yelled.

He looked happy to see her, and approached
her even though he was tired.

"Kobe, will you sign my jersey?"

He signs the jersey right across her stomach
right where I was.

Ever since then, I've practiced every day
shooting free throws
practicing cross-overs
trying to cook my opponents
shake them up and
make them stumble.
I wear a sweatband around my arm
like him.
My dream is to be drafted
to the NBA out of high school
like him.
I even have an "I love Jesus" necklace
that I hold and pray to
before my games:

Dear God, please give me
the same inspiration
that you gave Kobe

JANUARY 25, 2020

My first game
of the season, I am sweating from head to toe.
I feel like a snail sliding awkwardly
on the wooden gym floor, leaving a trail
of slime behind me.
My heart beats really fast
Road Runner plays drums in my ribcage
and my ears ring like church bells
loud enough to let me know what time it is

I am scared like a cat, but
I will not let it affect me;
I am trying to act brave like a bear.

I say my prayer before this game too
until I feel more confident, like I'm better
than everyone else on the team.

My mom is in the stands cheering me on
whistling like a bird circling its prey.
The opposing team looks worried
and so does BJ.
I feel like I came into the gym
with passion.

FIRST QUARTER

I bring up the ball, look at my coach
for the first play of the game
quick isolation
I dribble the ball in between
my legs, I pass the ball

to my teammate and run
straight for the hoop leaving
the person who is guarding me.
I shoot the ball.
Nothin but net.

SECOND QUARTER

25 to 15 and we're ahead.
I feel so tired but I
keep striving to win this game.
The other team is catching up.
BJ is shooting 3s like crazy
but I can't lose focus.

THIRD QUARTER

40 to 39 I get the ball
pass it to my teammate
for the easy 2, I get back on defense
BJ goes up for the ball.
My frustration takes over.
I push him.
Foul.
Now he gets 2 free throws
and BJ never misses a free throw.

FOURTH QUARTER

I can't lose this game.
I bring the ball down the court
and call a play called Iso.
I shift right so I can throw BJ off guard.
I show them how good I am
I do the famous Kobe Bryant fade away.

I turn around like a ballerina and shoot
the ball right away. Only...

...the ball rolls around the rim
and falls to the floor.

GAME OVER.

I walk to my mom and start crying.
It feels like something is off
I have never played like that before.
I go straight to bed
wondering what Kobe would think of me...

THE DEATH OF KOBE

The next day, I wake up at 10:58am.
I go downstairs,
eat breakfast, Cinnamon Toast Crunch
and turn on the TV to ESPN.
A normal Sunday.

I'm watching a rerun of Kobe's last game
against the Jazz 2016.
I study his fade-aways so that I
could never lose again.

Fade away
then the game is interrupted.
A newsman appears.
His face looks shocked.
He wipes his forehead
clears his throat
looks straight into the camera
straight at me
and says
"We interrupt this program to share that
Kobe Bryant has died in a helicopter crash."

My mouth drops and my eyes are wide open
my spoon falls to the floor
I feel like all the air
escaped from the living room.
I feel like I could die.
I turn to my mother and start to cry.
She holds me.

"Oh no, oh my God! This is horrible! Noooo!"
my mom says holding

back her tears.
She is holding her breath
Trying not to say anything because she knows
this is hard for me.
I know it is hard for her too.

"Mom, can I please be excused for a bit?"

I go to my room and punch the wall.
My knuckles sting as if bees swarmed them
my hands are red and covered in scratches.

I can't stop screaming inside my head at the pilot
wanting to place the blame
for taking away my idol.

I punch the wall again—
this time, a gaping hole—
and start crying
again.

Mom knocks on the door
"May I come in ?"
"Yes," I say.
She sits on the bed
I sit in a chair
and look at her
with tears in my eyes
like a forceful spout
like a spout
that can't stop
running.

"It's nobody's fault."
She says with a little shake in her voice
as if there were a mini earthquake

happening in my room.

"Sometimes bad things happen."

But why to HIM?

"Remember 3 years ago when you helped me
when I was sick and addicted?
You were so stressed,
but you told me about your dreams
that one day you would
go to college and play in the NBA.
And you helped see that we
had a future, made me realize
that drugs were not for me.
Just like when you overcame that—
you can overcome anything.

I'm listening, but not sure
I believe her yet.

"It will be OK
you will remind me of him—
of all his greatness
his passion
his dedication—
each and every day."

I hug my mother, but
I can't help but feel angry

Why did this happen?

I walk to the neighborhood court
I shoot 61 shots like Kobe did
in his last game.

THE BREAKDOWN

The next day, hanging out before school
the school bully, Justin, starts
talking about Kobe's death.
Justin has always been jealous
ever since sixth grade when I made
the team and he didn't.

"Did you hear about Kobe?"

    "Yeah. I'm mad that it happened."

"Bryant was kind of trash, though."

    "What did you just say?"
    I ball up my fist.

"I said Kobe was trash."

    "Oh so you think he's trash?
    I'll show you trash."

    I toss him onto the floor.

    "You're a bench player, my dude,
    you don't even know
    how to dribble."

Coach is walking by
and he grabs me. Says,
"Kobe, get off of him like that.
Go run fifty suicides"

Later, at lunch, I sit by my friend Troy.
"Are you okay," Troy asks,
noticing that I've been more quiet than usual.
"LEAVE ME ALONE," I say
harsher than I meant to
but I can't help it today.

Troy says, "I didn't mean to bother you—
you don't have to yell."
And it's true I don't have to yell
but my body can't help yelling
so instead I stand up and
BAM
I flip the table.

Everybody in the cafeteria gasps.
There's quiet
and then so much talking.

Dirk, the math teacher, sees me.
"Okay, settle down! Kobe can I talk to you for a second?"
He walks me to the principal's office.
On the walk, he puts his hand on my back
and says "Hey, I know it's a hard day
and you've got big feelings about it
but that's not the way. That can't be the way.
I need you to write an apology letter
and get it under control
you hear me?

I heard him—the sounds went in—
but that's about it.

Later that day
I walk to the gym.

Finally made it through classes, now practice.
Man I hate this school. The only thing
I like about it is the basketball team.
I feel like I don't belong anymore.
Without thinking
I kick
at a ball on the court
still trying to get out all this rage.

"Ahhh!" I hear Coach scream
and see blood dripping
from his nose.

"COME HERE!" he yells.
"That's it!
I am benching you
for the next four games!"

"WHAT?!" I say
"But those are all the games
leading up to state championships!"

"I don't care," he says
"the team's good without you.
We'll get there, Kobe."

I hear my name and think
about my passed legend.

It hits me all over again.
He's gone.

I run
to the bathroom, go into a stall
think about what I did, and cry.

I am angry, frustrated... and sad.

I come out and look in the mirror.
I see Kobe Bryant's reflection
Kobe Bryant comes out the mirror and says
"You're good at basketball
just don't let other people crawl into your skin.
Don't get yourself angry over me
because I'm close to you.
You see, legends never die.
When you play basketball
I'm right next to you.
When you're watching my last game
or my NBA Finals game
I'm even here in your name. Mamba out."

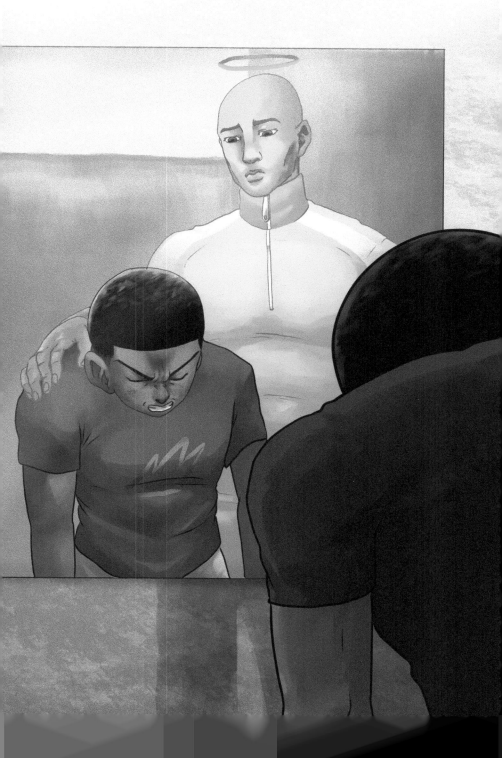

THINGS BEGIN TO CHANGE

I study the tapes of the opposing teams.
I go to the basketball court by my house
and practice the plays by myself.
Though I can't go to team practice anymore
I text my coach asking for the plays they reviewed
so that I can practice shooting.
I tell my coach about the progress
I'm making on and off the court.
I'm not going to miss that basket again.

Suddenly, all I can think about
is the State Championship game.
"We have to get this championship
so that I and all the other players
can work together and show our effort.
I remembered when Kobe took
the last shot and it went in
and he won the game.
"I think I can do that too."
I take the last shot of the practice,
And yell, "Kobe!"

It rolls around the rim for a minute
and then it goes in.

The next day, I wake up
and get dressed look in the mirror and say
"Last game of the season, but first championship!"
I've been practicing, but I feel anxious
I don't want to let myself down.

"I'm right next to you," I hear Kobe say

in my head
and I feel ready.

I go downstairs and see my mom
making pancakes and bacon.
She asks me if i am excited for the big game.
"Yea!" I say, "and ain't nothing
like a game day breakfast!"
She hugs me, and says
"I believe in you, my superstar."

I walk to school and see Justin, Troy, and Dirk.
They say good morning.
"Are you ready for the big game, Kobe?"
asks Justin
I fist bump him and just strut by
with my game face.

I have two classes before the game
and I don't do the work because
I'm too nervous. My leg shakes
up and down, and I keep checking
the clock. I look out the window
to see the bus parked at 10:00am
The bell rings and I run into the hallway
and into the coach, he says
"Kobe the game starts at 12:00pm today, so get packing."
I pack up, feeling pumped, and
kiss my Jesus necklace
for luck.

CHAMPIONSHIP GAME

When we arrive at the gym, I look at the stands.

I see Justin and Troy waving
at me, yelling "win this game!"

They yell like bears trying to get some honey.

I see BJ and he says "Let's call a truce
because we're both good at basketball
either way. Let's just be friends,"
and we shake hands.

His shake feels like a relief
like tylenol and a good nap.
I'm excited that he's here.

I see my Mom and she
is excited, grateful and proud.
I can tell because her face lightens
up like the sun coming up in the morning.
She is clapping like it is the 4th of July.
She holds up a sign that says
"K-O-B-E stands for superstar."
She stands, and I see
that she is wearing the jersey
Kobe signed.

I feel happy because
I remember all the struggles I went through
just to get to this point
my family and friends who were there for me
In that moment, I realize that Kobe is still with me

and that my community is right here.

Then I see our opponents
the Sierra Canyon Trailblazers.

"Listen up, Bobcats" Coach says
"Everybody, this is our final game. We need to strive to
    do our best.
I want you to remember that you all worked hard just to
    get here.
You all are talented and you're smart, and you have
    caring hearts.
You are superstars no matter what.
Kobe, even when you were suspended, you showed
    perseverance.
 Why don't you lead us in our chant?"
This made me feel special, I stand tall and begin

"Legends, Legends, never second
check the scoreboard and we're wreckin
Legends, Legends, it's no surprise
Legends, Legends never die!"

GAME TIME

I bring the ball up the court and pass it
to my teammate and sprint to the basket.
My teammate throws up a shot—
It doesn't go in. I shoot and it's good.
But that only brings the score to 54 to 60,
Trailblazers with a six point lead.
I see that and pass the ball
to my teammate who shoots it—
The ball rolls around the rim and goes in.
The score is now 56 to 60.
Back on defense
and I get a steal, drive to the basket
and dunk it! The score is 58 to 60.
Now back on defense, I look at my coach
for the play and he yells "Reset!" I freeze
the opponent and steal the ball,
pass it to my teammate for the layup.
Final minute, the score is tied 60 to 60.
I get a block at the rim and pass
the ball to my teammate, and
my teammate passes back to me
for the three.
Four seconds on the clock!
I smile and shoot—

The ball spins in the air
like a small Earth
and I realize everything
in this universe
is a cycle.
It tells me I am
who I believe in.

SURVIVOR

BY KHALIL BARNES

INTRO

My name is Ava.
Some people call me a freak
Think because I'm injured that I'm weak
Don't look further than the story that they seek.
People bully me, there's something there they don't see
Call me names constantly
like: Terminator.
Life-changing events should've hooked me to a respirator.
From the car crash,
I'm a survivor.

I always ask myself, "Why did it have to be me?"
I see my friends as no one, as just a bad memory.
Sometimes I wanna give up, but like the host of Jeopardy
said, "When you're in pain, take it one-day-at-a-time."
Now I'm hurting, in more ways than one,
and I've got to come up with a remedy.

Did I mention my dad was the one driving?

BULLYING TIME

I look at my watch

It's been 15 minutes
since I was last called a name.
I just got out of the hospital,
I stayed for a long while.
It was like being in the most boring class
It was like time took a day off
and never came back to work.

I'm thankful that I survived.

Thanks to my athletic body
I was able to live through the tragic accident
and get out of the hospital before doctors expected.

(Good thing I eat healthy, like my father
The father that almost killed me.
I guess I'm glad he gave me at least one good thing—
a habit we can be proud of)

From my human parts,
I most importantly still have my heart.
I have my left arm
My legs
My face...

But the rest?
Stolen, replaced.

I hoped for sympathy from my classmates
But with kids these days, asking for kindness

is like asking for peace—
It's just not happening
I was "Cyborg"
I was "Terminator"
I was everything but Me.
I ran to the bathroom stall
to cry my pain away.

I look at my watch

I knew coming back would not be easy.
I mean, half my body metal
and the other half still tender
I expected the bullying—
My school environment is hostile—
I just didn't know that it would be constant
Like the ticking of time
Like being on trial

I look at my watch

It felt like hours
It was only 15 minutes
I walk out to the hallway, empty
I remember it's a half day
and I'm ready to bolt.

But when I look to my left
I see Jake and his crew
sitting in detention, right next to the exit.
I freak out.
Those guys are extra *ugh*
They're the opposite of the library—
They're loud and know nothing.

I look at my watch

It's 11:15
In 15 minutes
They'll leave detention for lunch
so I will hide until then
and then make my escape
Like the times I spent reading
The Diary of a Wimpy Kid
I guess I see a lot of myself in him
Time after time

ROBOTIC

My torso is robotic,
going around my still human heart.
My right arm is robotic, too,
and my hand, a machine.
Where bones were crushed to smithereens,
my body was replaced.

My face, though, still human.
The eyes of my mother: blue.
The lips come from my mother, too.
Thin, never dry, naturally.
"Good" hair, in a Black neighborhood.
I don't do earrings.
I'm pale but Black.

My friends want to spray paint my robotic parts
to match my skin, to fit in.
I agree but also know it's not a fix—
The spray paint is washable.
It will stay on for a while but once water hits...
My disguise will come off instantly.

THE ACCIDENT

You're probably confused on how I got here.

I was walking by myself,
being impatient
(I have allegrophobia
It's extreme
It's a disability
It drove me to carelessly walk into the street,
the worst mistake of my life)

It was my father who crashed into me.

A cloudy and foggy day
colors that were hard to see
I was wearing my grey hoodie
He was speeding,
didn't stop at a red light
where I was crossing.

My dad has tinted windows—
you can only see the driver when you're up close—
and so up close
is when I noticed him
just before he hit me.

(He tried to stop
didn't he?)

A few people saw it
The neighbors saw it, too,
and they knew him,
he was very recognizable

in his expensive supercar.

And here's the thing
I can barely say:
He left and didn't come back.
My father drove away.

He tells me
that in his mind
he saw the police the minute he hit me.
He got overwhelmed—
he and the police, they have a history—
and he didn't even think,
He fled.

Eventually,
police arrested him
and asked for my perspective—
"Did he mean to do it? Why did he leave?"

All I could say was
I don't know
I was completely cracked
shattered
broken
with a $100,000 repair bill.

CONFIDANT

I am talking to Tracey.
She is calm, yet talkative.
She is patient and rarely gets mad.
She is sweet and funny.
She is a big explosion with a very long fuse.
She is my mom.
We are walking home.

She has seen all the bullying
since I've gotten the arm.
"I understand why you're being bullied,
and I know you don't deserve it.
I want you to be happy.
I don't want you to feel ashamed.
You don't have to listen to them."

She is my confidant.

"Thank you," I say while thinking to myself,
I want to be normal.
The journey to be normal
is extraordinary.

Remembering all I went through
Dreading what it would take to get a new arm:
Surgery, again, excruciating
Nevermind the $$$$$ pricetag
All that money I don't have
And do I really want to go under the knife
Again?
Horrifying flashbacks
Life-changing

Devastating
Like how people describe childbirth
12 to 16 hours
It's a blurry memory
I feel light-headed
remembering how light-headed I was.
I can see myself screaming
The fuzziness is a wall
stopping my clarity,
But I clearly remember
the pain.

VISITING DAD IN JAIL

There's a sigh.
I didn't want it to come down to this
Fearing the one thing I have to do
I'm scared, more like terrified
Wearing all grey again
Grey hoodie
Grey sweats
I have walked to the jail
First day of Spring Break

I'm regretting even coming outside.
The regret becomes greater as I get to the door
like all the bad things I have gotten away with
have come back to haunt me.
The door opening, sounds like my life ending
I explain myself to the guards
I can see that they can see
that I am terrified to be here.

This is my first time coming.
Talking through the glass in the visiting room
It feels odd and scary.
I'm already seated in my place behind the glass
when my dad walks up on his side and says,
"Hey kid, you're meeting someone?"

My dad is Black with a lot of hair, afro
He is tall and skinny
He is somewhat serious
and sad
as we talk through the visitation glass

"I'm looking for my father," I reply
He laughs
and takes a seat

He apologizes
Says he's sorry about what happened
He seems to know about the bullying
He has heard about it from Tracey
He explains that he knows
I'm not happy

I say to him,
"I'm trying but I can't get the words out."

"Take your time."

"The bullying. The name calling.
It's all too much for me.
I just want to stay home."

"I understand what problems you have."

"I just want YOU to come home."
(It's true, and it's not true, all at once.)

My dad looks at me.
"I can't explain how exactly,
but I can help."

I ask, in shock,
"Are you being released soon?"

"Another three years."

"Can you make it three months?"

He smiles a sad smile.
"Listen. Before I go,
remember that song I sung when you were little?"

"What song?"

"2, 4, 6, 8
You can decide your fate
5, 6, 7, 8
I'm gonna take away all your hate
2, 4, 6, 8
Scale of Justice, shift the weight"

I don't even know those lyrics.
"What?"

"I've got to go now,
Think about my words.
I love you. Be safe."

I'm walking home,
confused and scared.
It's warm outside
but for me it seems like a long cold night.

And as I walk
my brain starts to grow these ideas.

I think about the lyrics my dad sang
and how maybe it could lead me
to the place I need to be.

I run home to find the scale my father is talking about.

TIPPING THE SCALE

On his bedroom dresser,
my father has this Scale of Justice
The blindfolded woman you always see

2, 4, 6, 8,
Scale of Justice, shift the weight

Maybe this is what he was referring to?
I walk up to it
It never occurred to me touch it

I tip the scale...
and a trap door opens

Up through the dresser,
a computer rises and turns on.
Beside it?
$5,000 in large crips bills.

Whoa.

I type
2, 4, 6, 8
I feel like a hacker
Going through the mainframe
Looking into the data
Which holds such power
At this moment
It feels like I will explode

I scan through the computer for hours.
There are documents and so many emails:

Detailed architectural plans of banks

"Does your family know about Seattle?"

Links to newspaper articles

"Bro, I can't believe we almost got caught."

TV news clips about
West Coast bank robberies

*"You don't understand
how dangerous that would've been."*

I am beyond shocked

*"Lasers? You know you're not
flexible enough for that."*

All these years
I thought my father
was just a regular guy

*"If you tell anybody,
even your family members,
I WILL FIND YOU."*

Really, he's a criminal.

I let that sink in.

And apparently,
according to the schematics to the house
he's a criminal with a fortified safe
in the basement

full of cash.

Someone opens the front door.
My heart is pounding.
I put the Arm of Justice back,
and the computer dips back into the dresser,
the trap door closes,
everything goes back correctly.

Everything except my heart.

THE CHOICE

It's Tracey coming into the house.
I breathe a sigh of relief and
explain it all to her, in a rush:

I found a secret computer
I found a secret past
Dad has the money to pay for my surgery
It's here!
It's in cash, in the basement of our house
But there's a vault, and it's protected.
And Tracey, did you know this?
That he made this money illegally?
So if we use it, what happens?
Will the cops find out? Will they know that Dad stole it?
Will Dad be in jail... even longer?

I stop to catch my breath.

Tracey is shocked
Scared
Sad, mad
She always felt betrayed
that Dad hit me with his car
But now she is afraid
to make a choice:
Her child or her man?

"Where is it?" she asks.

There's a door
on the floor
of the kitchen.

It's the same color tile—
never seen it before—
but when you pull it up
there are stairs
going down, down, down.

My body is shaking
My legs feel like jello
Unable to move
All this time of desperation
and now just one thing stands in my way

There's a blue door with handles.
I pull it hard and open the door
Surprisingly colorful for a secret basement
Splashes of color that change like an aurora borealis
A place where rich people would talk about rich schemes
How they got their money and fame
I imagine Dad here, as a criminal,
and I'm angry.
And then I imagine him as just Dad,
giving his daughter clues to save her...
And how am I supposed to feel about that?

Then I see it: there's the vault!
There's a code panel,
and other high tech security—
Face recognition, laser, and traps
Rhythm patterns that taze you if you miss.

Tracey looks at me.
"Your robotic parts—
Do you have any superhuman strength?"

"I don't know," I say, "hopefully."

"Look!" says Tracey. "Your arm! It's glowing!"

And she's right—
My arm, it's warming
like there's a laser heating up.
And I feel hope, like maybe,
the power to fix this
is inside me.

I can burn through the vault!
I can disable the security!
I can get the money,
and make myself whole, but…
What about Dad?

(I imagine my dad
behind that visitation glass.
I see his sad smile,
and I see my reflection,
sad smiling back.)

I try to focus but I can't,
and I'm getting so, so, tired.
Tracey tells me, "Concentrate.
You got this, baby."

I get into a crouching pose
where I feel more comfortable.
I feel the energy going through my robotic body,
originating from my human heart.

"Do you know what great power you have?"
Tracey asks me,
and I say "No,"
but I mean YES

and when I say that truth again in my head,
I look down at my robot hand
and now it is bright, hot, red.

"Whatever you do,
Don't let anger get the best of you,"
Tracey says,
And I hear what she's saying
and suddenly feel quite calm.
Because I know that whatever I do,
It won't be out of anger
It will be out of love.

I've earned the right to do this
I've had the power all along—
2, 4, 6, 8
You can decide your fate

So I make my choice,
And I do.

HOOPS
AND HOPES

BY CHASE COOPER

THIS AIN'T NO FAIRYTALE

Once upon a time
there was a 14-year-old point guard
from Southeast DC named Brandon.
(That's me.)

And every day,
Brandon dribbled and passed and swished and dreamed...
even though his parents told him not to.

Until one day,
when Brandon learned the truth
about why they did not want to let him dream

And because of this,
everything began to change.

And because of this...

I wrote this story.

You ready?

ON THE LINE

The basketball is in my hand
Screaming hot as desert sand
I shoot the ball to update the score
But wait!
We still need more
15 seconds on the clock
It's their ball
We need more time, so I stall—

TIMEOUT!

There's a voice inside my head
making a loud, echoing shout
If only my parents were here—
to cheer!—
But no.
And even though
Granddad's by my side
when I see everyone else with their parents
It makes me feel...
a little dead inside.

(Yes there is joy
but I am only a boy
No parents to watch me play the game I enjoy?)

We need a three to tie
And—
You already know—
I make the shot!

But

Oh
Foot on the line
That's just a two
Too
few

What a shame
My shame
WE LOST

GENERATION GAP
(A CONVERSATION)

Granddad:
I'm proud of you, son. You did good. That's all that matters.
We'll get em' next time.

Brandon:
Yea, thanks Granddad. We were so close to winning! I feel
like it's my fault.

Granddad:
It's not your fault—you guys are a team. If it's your fault, then
it's everyone's fault.

Brandon:
Well I guess so. Good thing it's not the last game. I'll have a
chance to redeem myself.

Granddad:
Yea, well, let's get you home, kid.

Arrives home

Granddad:
Wait a minute, I wanted to give you something. I received
this gift when I was just your age, and I kept it just nice,
for my grandson, for you, and I want you to do the same.
It's a chain.

Brandon:
Yo! That's great, is it real gold? I mean not that it matters, I'm
grateful, you know. Thanks Granddad, I'll take good care of it.

Granddad:

I know you will, son. You can wear it around your neck or just keep it in your pocket, but never lose the chain, because it will remind you of me.

Brandon:

Thanks! I mean you never really give me anything, which is why I'm so shocked right now? Is there something—

Granddad:

No problem, but remember, when I'm gone, that chain will remind you of me, so if you lose it, or if you forget, then it's almost like you're going to forget me...

Brandon:

I hear you, Granddad, I won't lose it I promise.
(Swallows. Breathes in. Thinks about: "When I'm gone...")
Hey, you coming inside tonight?

Granddad:

I think it's best if I don't go inside, it's for everyone's good.

Brandon:

What do you mean by that Granddad?

Granddad:

Brandon, I said NO.

Brandon:

(Quiet.) Are you going to be OK walking home by yourself?

Granddad:

extreme cough

Brandon:

Are you sure you're OK?... Granddad? Granddad...

MEET MY PARENTS

I'm an only child,
So the "family unit"
Means me + Mom + Dad

There's Granddad, too
But he doesn't live with us
For reasons pretty old and sad

My parents are always busy
No time to watch me shine bright
When I first saw a basketball
it was like love at first sight

But my dad had other plans,
he thinks ball's a waste of time
I pour myself into my dream,
but he says it won't make me a dime
"What if there was no NBA?"
"What if you worked with me?" he always said
And when I realized he didn't support me,
it felt like my heart bled

My mom, she is doctor,
she likes to help others
And I admire that—
What are we without our mothers?
But she thinks ball is just a game
Not important, not the same
As following HER passion
Which also brings the cash in
She's always working hard it seems
Me realizing:

No time for her to watch me dream

So when I come home after that game
I don't say a single thing—
    Not about losing
    Not about Granddad
    Not about feeling it's all on me

Mom and Dad don't have time for breaks
Not even—the hard truth—for my sake.

ONE-ON-ONE

But you know who I do talk to?
Jordan.

(Hold up—
Have you met Jordan?
He's my best friend.
But we're arguing
Again
And that's on me
If it wasn't for my messed-up family
me and Jordan would be cool
but I'm selfish
Always going on
and on
(and on)
about my problems,
And do I ever ask Jordan anything?
About him?
For once?
You already know.
No.
So the next time we see each other
this is how it all goes down…)

***

Brandon:
Yo what's your problem,
my best friend once told me
to always solve them

Jordan:
Everything always goes your way, not my way
you talk free, like you driving on the highway

Brandon:
I know I can be selfish, like it's all about me
I've got issues, especially with my family

Jordan:
You never ask about how I feel
And around you I may seem chill
but trust me, it's a bigger deal

Brandon:
I hear that, man
I just need my best friend
I don't wanna argue—When's it gonna end?
It's like fire and thunder in one huge blend

***

I looked around
Everybody was clapping
I thought it was an argument,
but really we were rapping.

(I told you we was best friends.)

LITTLE DID I KNOW

The next day at school,
Everybody looking at me and smiling
My best friend came up to me
And he was smiling, too

"Yesterday after school,
someone recorded our rap battle
and posted on YouTube."

"Yo! That's crazy," I said. "How many views did we get?"

"30K," he said. A number bigger than I'd dreamed!
Which made it clear that if I listen
and hear what friends have to say
it only makes us stronger

So after I ask Jordan what's up with him
And hear about
    basketball problems
    how Coach won't give him time to play
    and how Madison won't give him the time of day
I tell him about the latest—
    Granddad and the chain
    the "When I'm gone"
    how he won't even come inside
    and how my own Dad don't care / don't know / don't see
Jordan sighs and says to me:
    Do ALL the men in your family
    need to learn about speaking and listening?
And I laugh, and I nod, and I say "yep."

Meanwhile
Little did I know...

FATHER FIGURES
(A CONVERSATION)

Dad:
Growing up, I couldn't choose my life.

Granddad:
I understand now, but there had to be a sacrifice.

Dad:
Why couldn't you sympathize? Instead you chose to terrorize.

Granddad:
Why so much blame? Now, son, don't criticize.

Dad:
All I wanted to do was socialize, exercise, organize,
    visualize... But when would you realize?

Granddad:
I wanted you to demand and apply, not sit here and cry. Now
    why lie? You make a lot of money.

Dad:
It's not about the money. Now why joke? This stuff isn't funny.

Granddad:
You're right, it's not funny, son, but you are so busy arguing
    with me that you don't even know what's going on with
    your own son.

Dad:
Leave my son out of this. Don't tell me how to be a father. It's
    not like you can talk. I try my best with Brandon, but I
    once had dreams, too.

Granddad:
What kind of dreams?

Dad:
Don't worry about it, and I am sick of this. It's best if you leave.

Granddad:
Begins to grab his chest as he walks out of the door
Goodnight, John.

Dad:
Yeah, whatever.

DEATH IN THE FAMILY

About an hour later
Dad gets a call
He looks like he has seen a ghost
I've never seen him look so worried

Granddad...

My Mom is just as upset as Dad
Even though it's not her father
She can't be happy when Dad isn't
I hear her crying quietly
I was never a loud crier either
To hear news like this makes me feel
not like me

Granddad is sick...

My mind fills with random thoughts...
What can I do?
Is it my fault?

Granddad is sick in the hospital...

Dad is speeding so much it feels like I need two seatbelts
He has this look of guilt in his eyes
A look where he knows he's done something wrong
and it may be too late to make up for it

As soon as we arrive to the hospital,
both of my parents rush out of the car
We enter and my Dad yells,
"What room is my father in?

What room is my father in?!"

The nurse at the front desk walks towards us and says,
"Sir, I am going to need you to calm down,
and tell me your father's name."

He tells her

The nurse checks the sign-in sheet,
and tells us the room number
We practically run down the hall
before it's too late

Once we get to the room,
I can't help but stop and stare
Granddad is in the hospital bed
His face is dry and rough,
and he looks at me like he needs to say something
Almost like he knows his time on Earth
is coming to an end.

"You can wear it around your neck," he says,
and his voice is so scratchy
like he has been coughing all day,
"Or just keep it in your pocket."

"What?" says my Dad,
But I know exactly.

"Hey, son," Granddad says, turning to my Dad,
"Everything bad that happened between us?
Try not to let it happen all over again."

His voices begins to fade
I cannot help but say—

"Don't leave us!"

And he says, "I'm not.
When that chain is near you, I am near you,"
And then, "Don't forget... th..."

And today was the day
that my Granddad died.

SO FAR

I don't know where to start.

As of right now,
I am feeling
different emotions.

I am feeling
upset
angry
guilty
drained
but most of all
I am distracted

Yesterday at basketball practice it was like I forgot all
my drills.

I couldn't catch,
nor pass
and most of all
I couldn't score.

People have been talking to me,
and I haven't been listening
because I keep my mind on one thing all day.

You know.

During all of my classes,
it feels like time flies by.

At lunch and at home,

I don't eat much,
even though everyone says
I should.

Usually when I go home now,
I try my best to not talk to anyone
until I am ready.

So far,
I am not talking.

THAT'S WHAT FRIENDS ARE FOR

Jordan:
Hey man.

Brandon:
Hey.

(It's after basketball practice that week,
and I still haven't said anything to Jordan,
because if I could talk to anyone,
it'd be him,
but still,
not yet.)

Jordan:
Your parents told me, but they assumed that you had already
    told me...
I'm really sorry.

(Quiet.)

There is no point in me asking if you're OK because I know
    you're not.

(Quiet)

And I also know I can't really help you.

Brandon:
(I'm holding a ball
and I bounce it hard a few times
because what am I supposed to say
to him, to that?)

Jordan:
But what I can do is tell you to talk to your Dad. He is just as
    upset and angry as you are. He was your granddad, but he
    was your father's father.

Brandon:
(These are the things I want to say:
I'm surprised they called you.
At home I just go straight to my room,
and no one bothers trying to talk to me
even if I don't want them to.
And sometimes I know I want them to.)

 (This is what I do say:)
I don't think that would be a good idea.

Jordan:
Well at least try to say something to him, he's still your fath—

Brandon:
I know he is my father, you don't have to be so worried about me!
anger sparks

Jordan:
I do, I do have to be worried about you. The reason I am
    talking to you now is because if you're not talking to your
    parents, and you're not talking to me, you're not talking to
    anybody. Am I right?

Brandon:
(Quiet)

Jordan:
Oh!, and you should really eat something. I've noticed at
    lunch you barely touch your food.

Brandon:

(Quiet, but then Jordan shakes his head and starts to leave so
    I gotta say something—)

Yeah, OK, I hear you. Hey, what's for lunch today?

Jordan:

Bread with jam, sunbutter, and celery sticks...

Brandon:

(Makes a face.) Nevermind I'll wait until I get home to eat.

Jordan:

(Laughs) Make sure you do...

And hey? Don't forget to talk to your dad.

FATHER-SON TALK

Today I'm excited
Excited for the first time in a long time
because today we only have a half day of school.

Which means right when school is out
I will either go home and watch TV
or go to the basketball court.
Either way, a perfect afternoon.

And when the bell rings
My stomach growls
(No lunch again today)
And so I know: it's TV for me,
and the couch, and a sandwich.

When I arrive home, I see my Dad's car outside.

Stomach drops.
Why's he here?

I walk in and go straight to the kitchen
It seems like I am hearing extra footsteps
but they are just mine. Right?

I finish making my sandwich, and there they are again.
Footsteps. Creaks.
Are they above me?

I go for the stairs and see that the attic is open.
The rickety pull-down stairs are visible, pulled-down.

I've never been up to the attic

I was allowed to but I never wanted to.
The lights are on?
I guess I'm going today.

I walk slowly up the stairs,
and when I get up there,
I see my Dad,
with a paintbrush.

I am confused.

Me:
Dad? What are you doing with a paintbrush?

Dad:
(Startled.)
I thought you were supposed to be at school, what happened?
(Clearing his throat.)
What else would I be doing with a paintbrush? I'm painting.

Me:
It's a half day so they let everyone out early.
(I walk further in, and I cannot believe it.
The whole attic is full—
of paintings.)

Whoa. Is this you, Dad?
You did all of this?
When?
You never told me you could paint.

Dad:
You're right. I never told you.
(Deep breath.)
But yeah, I wanted to be an artist when I was younger, about

your age. Your Granddad had other ideas though. He thought I should do something that actually helps me make money.

Me:
But you're really good at it.
Too good.
Does Mom know about this?

Dad:
No, I didn't know when to tell you guys.

Me:
But Granddad knew... And he didn't let you...

(Something inside me twists and changes. Was that the same Granddad I knew?)

Dad:
Look, your grandfather was some man, he made me who I am. I understand why he did what he did, pushed me into the family business. But I also think he regretted it, in the end... Why do you think he always showed up for you? Supporting you? I think he knew to make up for his mistakes...

Me:
(Fingers rubbing Granddad's gold chain. Thinking.)

Dad:
And he was right. To support you. I don't like who I am if I'm not supporting my only son. I feel bad about it, conflicted all the time. So I paint, and each painting shows my way of expressing how I feel.

Me:

I wish I would have known earlier.
I blamed you for so much...
I really like your paintings, Dad.

Dad:

It's OK, son. And thank you. How about this: from now on,
you support my dreams, and I'll support yours.

Me:

For real, I am not sure if I want to play basketball anymore,
after what happened to Granddad. It's so hard to get out
there and not to see him in the bleachers, you know?

Dad:

I do know.

Me:

Anyway, thanks Dad, and you should show people your
paintings more often. They are pretty good for a business
man.

Dad:

(Laughing.) Thanks, son.

THAT NIGHT

That night,
I was angry.
I was sad.
I was confused.
For a second, I wanted to quit everything,
basketball mainly...

Because it all felt like too much:
    The Granddad I didn't know
    The Granddad I did
    "When I am gone."

And just before I fell asleep
and had decided to quit the team
Dad popped his head in and said,
"Your next game—can I be there?
In Granddad's seat?"

And I said "Sure,"
and like I told you in the beginning,
Everything changed.

GAME TIME

Time for the basketball to be back in my hand
Still hot as desert sand
But this time it's the sands of time
Time to dribble and pass and swish and dream
Time to get this big win with my team

But guess who has the same dream?
The other team

Mom and Dad are here
Ready to cheer
They took his spot
In the stands, not in my heart
But still
I'm that boy with the joy
Again

Now into overtime
And it's my time
My time to shine
11 seconds on the clock
I have to take the shot
Or maybe not
Granddad's voice in my head
It's like he's next to me
Telling me to shoot the three
TIME
TIME
TIME
I am nervous like I committed some crime
And this time—
No foot on the line—

The ball goes in!

And there's a win.
!

(But still, something missing.)

I wore his gold necklace to remind me of Granddad
And even though I won the game—
I still feel sad

Hard to feel all the feels
When part of you is gone

But then
The crowd noise reaches me
Screams and shouts preach me
My Dad's voice rising, over everyone:
THAT'S MY SON!
And I look him in the eye
As he runs onto the court
Arms wide, face open
Yes
I am

ZIM AND
THE QUEST FOR
THE CLOAK

BY JOSIAH OUABO

SICK

Hi. My name is Zim. Zimmerman Brogdon, but you can call me Zim. I'm just a 15-year-old boy who lives with his grandmother.

It wasn't always just me and Grandma. I obviously had a mother, but she died giving birth to me. All I have left of her is a white feather that she always wore in her hair. My mother was said to be light-skinned and youthful. Apparently I have her same thick lips and her green, green eyes. My grandma says that I look most like my dad, though. I have his dark, curly hair and his milk-chocolate skin. But he left us when I was little, so I don't remember what he looked like, either.

So I live with my grandmother.

And now, she's dying.

She is sick with Avian Scarring.

Avian Scarring is the worst possible disease you can think of. It's the rarest, most dangerous, most painful sickness out there. It causes: blurred vision, walking difficulty, hallucination, gum pain (not in all cases), coughing (uncommon)... and, eventually, in almost all cases, death.

Grandma only has one month to live.

Avian Scarring cases have started to increase over the years. The disease comes into effect fifty years after the wound is inflicted—that is, if the victim doesn't die on the spot. The way you get the wound is if you are cut with the Life Limit, a special type of demon sword that only the demon captains use. Fifty years ago, we were at war.

My grandmother was slashed, right across the cheek. She will not tell me the story.

But she did tell me a legend—it's about "The Cloak of Revival." The Cloak is said to be the cape of an angel, able to cure any wound, external or internal. No one has ever been able to complete a quest to recover it. Yet. But I know it would help make my grandmother well again. It would help bring sickness to its very end. And that's a price I am willing to pay.

I need to embark on this journey.

THE JOURNEY BEGINS

My grandmother sees me packing up. "Where do you think you're going, young man?"

"I'm going over to the woods to camp," I lie.

"Well you better come back tomorrow by noon!"

"I will." I still don't have the guts to tell her that I'm going off to find the Cloak.

"I'm just playing with you, boy, I know that you are going to the Cloak," she says.

I stop in my tracks.

"You may be able to beat me physically, but my eyes are sharper than a knife. Even with this blasted disease I can still see that compass and those clothes..."

How could I be so careless?

"I know I can't stop you. But if you must go, then I must help," Grandma says. She gets up and stretches her thin arms.

"What? No. Get back in bed!" I object.

She waves me off and walks over to a painting of me with a pirate hat with a wooden sword. She looks at it then looks at me. Then sighs. She tilts the painting to a ninety degree angle and rips it off the wall!

"What the heck? I loved that picture," I say.

Grandma shrugs. She presses the wall where the painting was and the wall caves.

It was a secret door all this time!

Inside there is a room full of different types of weapons: axes, swords, knives, and hammers. If you could think of it, it is there.

"Pick what you want," Grandma says. "There's more than enough to go around."

I walk around and pick up a dagger.

"That's good, but you need a long range weapon as well, like a throwing ax or bow and arrow. If you meet someone

who is good at close range then long range is the way to go."

I pick up a white bow and begin to aim at a target posted on the opposite wall. I shoot and the arrow misses by ten feet. Grandma sighs and walks up to me.

"Well, you're better than I thought you would be… but you still have much to learn."

She proceeds to give me pointers on how to hold the bow, and how to release the arrow. I get better, to the point where I can hit the target. She then teaches me how to use a dagger and other throwable weapons.

"Well, with the amount of time we have, I won't be able to turn you into a master, but at least you're good enough to begin this journey," she says.

I turn to hug her, but she holds her hand out. In her hand is a piece of rolled-up paper.

"This is a map for the route to the Cloak. My friend made it. He attempted the journey twice. The second time, he never came back. I kept his map to remember him. I feel like you'll need it."

I take the map. I never knew that Grandma's friend had tried to find the Cloak. But then again, I never knew that Grandma could throw knives, either. She is full of surprises.

Grandma puts her hand on my arm. "I must tell you something before you leave," she says. "You have powers beyond your dreams. You can soar higher than any eagle."

I stare at her blankly. "What do you mean?"

"You shall find out soon enough."

"Well, thank you, Grandma. For everything."

I hug her and walk out of the house. I wipe away a tear and begin my journey.

A RUDE AWAKENING

I head out and look at the map. First I must go to the swamp. Great. For three whole days I walk, and finally the terrain changes from sticky marshy bog to a wide green forest. By the time I make it out of the swamp, it's clear I am unprepared in so many ways. Like food. I brought granola bars, but not enough, and already I am running out. I attempt to catch rabbits, using Grandma's bow and arrow tips, but time and time again, I fail.

What am I going to do?

For now, I quit and head toward a nearby cave. I know I can't make any good decisions without sleep. So I take a nap for a while until I am awakened by a growl...

Bear.

I grab my bow and arrow and I shoot and it grazes the grizzly's cheek. It roars in anger and charges at me.

Bear!

I shoot again and again until the bear smacks me—WHACK!—into the wall of the cave. I don't feel the pain because of all the adrenaline. I shoot again and again, but I miss. Finally, when the bear is in striking range, I fire. The arrow goes into its eye and the bear roars in agony. I shoot it a few more times in the neck for good measure and wait while the breathing stops. My heart is pounding.

At least now I have food for the week.

I pull out my knife and skin the bear for its meat. And this time, I fall into deep, deep sleep.

DRIED OUT

The next day I pack the meat and head out. I exit the forest and reach an oasis, seeing the desert in the distance. And then I see her—a girl in nomad clothing, gathering water in some jars. Her two camels are tied up nearby, grazing on the grass.

I walk to the oasis to drink the water, keeping my head up to see what this girl will do.

Not like a stalker, but cautiously. It doesn't matter—she ignores me. So after having my fill of water, I go to a nearby tree and sit under it, basking in its shade until I fall asleep.

Night falls, the sun rises, and I wake up to find the girl still sleeping. She's there with her camels, under a nearby tree. I'm curious about her but have no time for distraction. It will be hot in the desert, so I must set out early. I start walking and continue for hours.

The sun beats down. No mercy. I walk until my tongue cracks and my throat aches. I reach for a water canister, but it is already empty. *Dang it!* I keep walking, tired and battered, and soon, I pass out from exhaustion.

Is this how I die? I wonder. *I didn't even get to save Grandma.*

But suddenly a splash of water cools my face. I gasp and look around, seeing the girl from the oasis standing over me. I sit up and shake the water out of my hair.

"Thank you," I say. *Who are you?* I wonder.

The girl is tan with a turban wrapped around her head. She has smooth skin and deep brown eyes. I stand up and look down. She's shorter than me by about three to four inches.

Without saying a word, the girl gives me a camel and I follow her towards a nearby group of tents that I hadn't even seen in my delirium. A man with a mean face looks in our direction. The man starts stomping, face red with anger, almost bursting. He is stocky and looks like an ox.

"Where were you, Vanessa!? I told you not to leave the campsite for any reason.

And who is this?" he asks, pointing at me. "First you leave without permission, then you bring OUTSIDERS to our camp."

The ox-man towers over me. "Get out of my camp right now," he threatens.

"No," Vanessa says. It's the first word I've heard her speak. Her voice is quiet but firm. "I brought him here because he doesn't have anything to survive out there. If we let him out, he'll die."

The man looks at her, looks at me, shakes his head, and backs away. "He's *your* responsibility," he says.

"Yes, Father," she replies.

That ox-man is her father?! I think. *Who is this girl?*

TAKE ME WITH YOU

I stay at their camp for about three days, recovering my strength and gathering supplies. I collect food and water for my next three days—it's all I can carry. The whole time I am there, no one speaks to me. Not the girl, not the others, and certainly not her father. She watches me and brings me food and water, but that is all. I spend my days thinking about Grandma, and the Cloak. I study my map. I wonder if I can make it.

Finally on the day I'm ready to leave I begin to walk away from the camp, not looking back. Suddenly I hear, "Where do you think you're going?"

I turn around and see Vanessa staring at me with two camels at her side.

"It's none of your concern," I say.

"Take me with you," says Vanessa.

She doesn't talk to me for days, and then she wants to go with me?! I'm sure she'll slow me down. No way.

"No," I say. "Your father—he'd be worried sick. You have to stay here. And anyway, what can you do to keep us alive? You're not a hunter. You're a nomad."

Vanessa turns red with anger.

"Oh, I can keep us alive."

She shifts her clothing to show a sword hanging from her belt. "See this? I don't think you even know how to use it. I could kill you with it right now... and you'll never get to your goal. Or, you can take me with you, and you might just have a chance of surviving."

She climbs onto her camel, looks back and says, "You coming?"

I laugh nervously and start riding.

GASPING

After a while, it starts getting dark. Vanessa pulls out a torch from her bag to illuminate the pitch black wasteland.

"So where are you going that you risked your life wandering through the desert?" she asks.

"Are you sure you want to know?"

"Duh, I'm asking."

"Have you heard about The Cloak?"

Vanessa chuckles. "I can't believe I am following a madman. You know that people *have died* trying to even get a glimpse of that thing. They don't even know if it exists. We'll die before we even reach it."

"Well, it's a good thing you came along."

"It is, actually," she says. "And besides, I have my own reasons to make this journey."

I wait for her to say more, but she doesn't. She's a girl of mystery for sure.

We continue on the road and keep trotting.

~

Over the next few days we travel from desert to mountain range to swamp. Every environment brings a new challenge. We are running low on meat, so I attempt to go hunting.

Vanessa stays behind at camp while I struggle through the foliage, hacking at vines to clear a path. Suddenly I hit something tough and freeze in my tracks. The "vine" I thought I cut is actually a large green anaconda.

Uh oh.

The snake starts circling, staring at me, while I slowly get the bow off my shoulder. I'm trying not to make any sudden moves, but that's the wrong choice—this snake is *fast*. Before I know it the anaconda has coiled around my legs. Then my waist. I grab my dagger and try to stab, but the snake coils around my chest, squeezing my ribs with crushing force. I start wheezing, gasping for air. And then? It all goes black.

I guess I'm dead, again.

At least I'll be able to meet Mom?

BOOM

"Wake up, wake up, WAKE UP."

I jolt awake, hitting my head on something hard.

"Ow!" Vanessa yells. Oh. That hard thing was her head.

I take a deep breath. I'm breathing! I'm alive! I look around and see the giant snake beside me on the ground, a deep red gash between its eyes.

"How did that happen?"

"I killed it," Vanessa says, still rubbing her head.

"There's no way," I say. "Something else must have killed it. A monkey, maybe? Also, you were at the camp. There is no way you could've come in time."

I get up and swipe some of the mud off of my pants and get up. But this time, finally, she explodes.

"IF YOU THINK I DIDN'T DO IT, THEN LOOK AT MY SWORD!"

I look down to see her bloody sword in her grasp.

"Huh," I say. "Okay, maybe you did. Thank you, I guess... So if that's all, let's get a move on."

Vanessa, red with fury, knuckles white, grabs my arm and pulls me down to her level. She slaps me across the face.

"Wake up! If you think that you can do all of this by yourself, then go ahead! I won't stick around with someone who doesn't trust in their comrades!"

boom

"Vanessa?"

"No, I won't listen to what you have to say."

"Vanessa, I'm sorry. Let's go back."

Boom

"Vanessa, come now!"

BOOM

An enormous shadow passes over us, and we look up. And there, towering over us is...

A GIANT

Ten meters tall with marshy green skin, and such a foul stench that it stings the nose. I've heard about Giants from my grandmother, but I've never seen one in real life. How I wish that was still true.

"I, sleep. You, loud. I, MAD," the Giant roars. He punches at the ground and it creates havoc, with trees uprooting and animals scrambling. I pull Vanessa to shield her from the debris. When we fall, I am above Vanessa and I look away, blushing.

"Look, there!" Vanessa yells, pointing. "Could it be…?"

And that's when I see it. A sword, hanging on a rope from the monster's neck like a medallion. It must be. "The Life Limit!"

I get up and unsheath my dagger, ready to strike the behemoth. I dash forward with Vanessa close behind, and then turn and boost her up to attack. She attempts to slice at the giant and makes a shallow gash. The Giant laughs and stomps, making the earth jiggle like jello. I keep trying to stab at his feet but the Giant kicks me away, knocking the breath out of me. Then he swats Vanessa so hard she bangs her head on the ground with a loud *thwack*.

The Giant bends over an unconscious Vanessa and laughs. He scoops her up. Then he walks over to me. "You, awake?"

"What does it look like?" I say through gritted teeth.

"Yay, you awakie. Good, you with me." The Giant picks me up and starts to walk away.

WHITE FEATHERS

We end up outside of a cave with a huge boulder. Shivers go down my spine as I feel the ominous energy oozing from the cave. The Giant rolls back the rock and enters.

I can't see anything in the darkness. Then, as my eyes adjust, shapes appear. There are bones—human bones—here and there, scattered across the dirty room. In the middle of it all sits a super-sized seat, like a throne.

The Giant gets ropes and begins to tie us up. For a guy with big fingers, he sure is good with his hands. When he walks away, I struggle to reach for my dagger and finally get a grip. While his back is turned, I start to cut the ropes that bind us. The Giant is trying to build a fire.

"Fire, work!" he yells. Finally, he gets it started.

Three ropes left.

The Giant gets some shrubbery to fuel the flames.

Almost there.

The Giant gets up and starts walking back to us.

One left.

The Giant bends down right in front of me.

DONE!

I throw the dagger straight through his eye. The Giant screams in agony and curses while I untie Vanessa, who was finally awakened by the roars. She runs to the fire and gets a flaming stick. She runs back to the Giant. She puts the fire directly on the skin of the Giant and makes sure the Giant knows it. He screams. He opens his one good eye and grabs a giant rock, hurling it towards Vanessa.

It's going to hit her.

You can see the fear plastered on Vanessa's face.

She's too far. Why can't I do anything?! She's always protecting me, and now I can't repay her.

"NOO!" I scream, and suddenly wings spread across my back. I sweep in and pull Vanessa from the line of fire. The rock just misses us, shattering against the cave wall. I open my eyes to see Vanessa in my arms, and put her down.

"I didn't know you could fly," she says.

"Neither did I!"

I look at my white feathered wings. *Mom?* I wonder. But there's no time to think, because the Giant is roaring, coming straight at us. I flap my wings and fly, straight at the Giant. I jerk the dagger out of his eye and then fly around and around his neck, slashing uncontrollably. The Giant swings his arms around, looking like a cat trying to catch a laser. And then finally I slice my target—the necklace—and the sword falls to the ground, clanking before being snatched up by Vanessa.

"I got it!" she yells. She pulls the sword out of its scabbard. The katana is a mellow black that shines from the flickering of the fire. She turns around and charges forward. She slices at the back of the giant's knees—and the Life Limit cuts straight through.

The Giant looks down in surprise to see his severed leg. He falls with a colossal BOOM.

I fly down and retract my wings. Vanessa goes up to the head of the Giant and raises her sword to end him, but he cries out: "Wait! There is something you need to know. You will never get out of here alive."

"What do you mean?" Vanessa questions.

"You really think I'm the final boss? I'm flattered," he says with a gasp and a chuckle. "I am nothing compared to my boss. You will get flattened just by his aura alone."

How strong is this boss? I wonder.

"Zim! You're shaking," Vanessa says.

"Huh?" I look at my hands and hold them down.

"Who is your boss?" Vanessa asks.

The Giant smiles. "Oh," he says in a fading voice, "you'll find out."

And then his eyes go flat. Vanessa checks his pulse and turns to me.

"Dead," she says.

TAKER OF LIFE

We take a quick break to recover our strength, and then proceed to search the rest of the cave. We rummage through, looking for anything that could be the Cloak. We look up, under, wall to wall, but the only thing we find are the toe clippings of the giant. Gross.

I climb onto the Giant's throne and look around. Nothing. Just as I'm about to hop down, I notice a slight shimmer of bronze through the crack of the seat. I call Vanessa over to help me lift it up. We both pull up with all of our strength, and finally it gives. Below us is an open chest, full of different weapons: long swords, bows and quivers, axes, knives, hammers, and more. And on top of them is a note:

> If you're reading this note, that means that you have defeated the Giant and have received the Life Limit. For your valor, you may choose any weapon from this chest. But, choose wisely, for you may never see this chest again. If you leave now, you can avoid death. But if you continue, you will not survive.
>
> Good luck,
> the Dwarves

We look at each other, then look back at the paper.

"We need to get out of here now!" Vanessa says in a quivering voice.

"We still need to get the Cloak, Vanessa. We can't go back now."

"Are you serious? We barely beat that Giant and are still recovering. Do you really want to die? I didn't come here to watch someone throw their life away. I can't lose another..." Her voice catches in her throat and she looks away.

"Another?" I ask. "Who else—?"

But I am interrupted by a loud rumble. We stop arguing and look around, trying to find where the sound is coming from.

"I'm telling you we need to get out of here," Vanessa says. "I have a bad feeling—"

Suddenly the walls around us crumble to reveal a sleeping dragon. Its magnificent size makes the Giant look like a mere child. As it sleeps, its silver scales rise up and down, up and down. There is a ruby in its forehead, glistening in the dim light.

The dragon opens its eyes. It yawns, revealing its gigantic sharp jaws, and focuses its attention on us. "So you are the insolent brats who beat Bob?" the dragon bellows. His booming voice echoes through the crystalized cave.

Bob? I guess that's the Giant's name. For an intimidating guy that name makes him sound like a teddy bear...

The dragon snaps his fingers and the room suddenly lights up. The cave is twice as big as the one we just emerged from.

"Who are you, and where is the Cloak?" I ask, shaking.

"Isn't it disrespectful to demand I identify myself before you even share your own name?" the dragon says, releasing a little bit of bloodlust.

We want to move but our bodies refuse. I eye the treasure chest of weapons below me. A sharp, shiny axe catches my attention...

"But to answer your question, my name is Qote, The Taker Of Life. The only way out of here is to defeat me. Which is unlikely."

"Well," I say, "I guess we have no choice."

DRAGON FIGHT

I grab the axe and start running at Qote. He swats me to
the side. I unleash my wings and swing the axe, dragging the
blade across his scales, but it barely leaves a mark. Instead
it makes a sound like someone scratching their nails on a
chalkboard. The horrible sound makes Vanessa wince, and
she leaps into action. She slashes back and forth with her
new sword, forcing Qote to dodge.

"Ah, the new wielder of the Life Limit. What a surprise.
And scrappy! Just like your mother. Such a pity she was so
ill..." Qote says with a grin.

"How do you know about my mother?" Vanessa asks.

"Oh, your mother was one of my favorites... Such a fighter,
even when she was sick! She told me she would capture the
Cloak and get well so she could watch her daughter grow up.
That must be you! Such a shame," he chuckles. "You humans
really are fools. You think you can challenge me?! Your
mother learned. The hard way."

Vanessa is looking down at the ground. I can't see
her eyes but her clenched fists and her breathing tell me
everything. She is mad.

"You bastard!" Vanessa screams as she flails around.
Qote flings his tail, slamming her into the roof. I catch her.

"Calm down, Vanessa," I say. "You're letting him win.
Don't listen to him. We won't get out of here alive if we are
not focused. You have to kill this thing—not for me, but
for your mom. Avenge her. Now get up and let's kill this
overgrown lizard."

"Overgrown lizard! Whoa whoa whoa. Can't you have
a little respect for the one who is about to end your life?
I should kill you where you stand," the dragon sceams.
Suddenly a mountain of crystals comes crashing down on us.
We dodge backwards and escape the avalanche by the skin

of our teeth.

I grab Vanessa by her shoulders and take off, flying around the dragon's neck, ready to blitz. Vanessa slashes with her sword, but even though it is the Life Limit it's hard to cut through the scales. She is only able to make flesh wounds.

"Crystals, crystals, you've run out of time. Trying so hard for something you won't find. Crystals, crystals do you hear my call? The one in my head is the best of them all," Qote sings.

The dragon swings his sharp claws in the air, scraping my back all the way to my upper ribs. I yell in pain as I fall to the ground. I look at the wound and see that my right wing is gone. I curse under my breath. "You're going to have to do this by yourself, Vanessa. I can't fly anymore."

Vanessa nods and turns around just as the dragon's giant tail comes crashing down, ready to flatten her. It looks like it's the end—I see Vanessa close her eyes against her inevitable death. NO! Something inside me surges with power.

The next thing I know, Vanessa is opening her eyes to me holding up the tail. I don't even know how I stopped it. I hear Grandma's voice in my head: *You have powers beyond your dreams...*

With blood dripping down my face, I say, "I guess we're even." I tighten my grip on the tail and roll over the dragon, exposing his soft underbelly. "Now go and kill this thing!" I say.

Vanessa jumps up and drags the Life's Limit across Qote's belly, slicing him open. Quote screams in pain and Vanessa jumps off.

"Vanessa, come here!" I yell. She runs to me.

"Do you remember that mumbo jumbo he was saying earlier about crystals? He said 'the one in my head is the best of them all.' That's his ruby!"

Vanessa's eyes widen as she catches on. "What if we destroy his ruby—that could be the source of his power?!"

Vanessa says. She wheels around and faces the dragon. "How about we finish this, you giant freak!" she yells. "If you're so big and bad, come at me on my level. You should be able to beat me in any conditions."

"Oh really? You have some nerve for someone who was getting folded around earlier." Qote lowers his head down to where Vanessa is. Vanessa suddenly swipes down, so fast that even Qote is surprised. The sword cuts cleanly, right through the ruby.

The gem falls out of Qote's head all the way to the floor, cracking on impact. Qote jumps back. He looks at us and shivers as if someone has lowered the temperature down to zero degrees. Spikes of crystals slowly encase his body.

"Noooo! This is impossible!" Qote shrieks. "I'm the Taker of Life, I live forever!"

We watch as Qote slowly turns into a pile of ash.

HEALING

We sit there, panting, staring at the mound of dragon dust. We're both stunned to be alive. We beat the boss! But wait. Where is the Cloak?

I walk into the pile of ash and rummage around. *This darn Cloak better be here. I did not risk my life for nothing!*

We both dig through the ash until our hands and faces are covered. My heart is sinking and I am just about to give up when suddenly I get a glimpse of blue amidst all that gray gray gray. I snatch it up. In my hands I get my reward: blue and shiny, impossibly light. Suddenly I feel my drowsiness go away, my muscles no longer sore. My right wing heals and sprouts anew, almost as if we have rolled back time.

I motion for Vanessa to come over and hand her the cloak. Instantly her cuts and bruises vanish and color returns to her face. Tears run down my cheeks and I get on my knees. "Finally, we did it!" I shout. "The Cloak is ours!"

For a moment we both just hold the Cloak, feeling its power. I imagine my grandmother, un-withering and rising up out of her pain. And I feel lighter, too. It's like the emptiness I used to feel, carrying around the absence of my parents—it's gone. How could emptiness feel so heavy?

I can see Vanessa is imagining something too, but her face is sadder. I know now why she set out on this journey, how she was also seeking healing. I hope the Cloak can help her with her loss, too.

Vanessa looks off at the horizon. "How are we going to go home?" she asks.

I flap my wings. "Well, thanks to Thing One and Thing Two here, we can get there in a few hours." She smiles and hangs onto me as I fly off towards the oasis.

OASIS

Soon enough, we reach the oasis. From above, I see some of the kids outside playing. Suddenly one of them spots me and points. Some of them run and get their parents, and they all look up. They watch us glide down to the ground and land. Vanessa gets off of my back and the people gather around us. They keep looking at me in awe, and some of the kids even touch my wings.

Suddenly, Vanessa's dad exits his tent and begins to sprint towards us. *This is going to be hard to explain.* "Inside. Right now. Both of you!" he yells.

I retract my wings so I can fit through the narrow entry, and we walk into the tent.

"Sit down," he says. We do as we are told. Vanessa's dad is fuming. If he was an ox before, now he is now a ravenous elephant about to charge through anything that moves.

He takes a deep breath, trying to calm himself down. "Where were you, and why did you leave without my permission?" he asks in a deep but soft voice. For some reason this is scarier than him yelling like before.

"W-we were adventuring, Father. We came back safe, though."

"Okay, but that doesn't explain why you went out without permission on your own!"

"But Zim was there with me."

"Oh yeah, don't think I forgot about you, young man. You took my daughter without my blessing for almost a month. The audacity! And how do you have wings? That's impossible. Are you even human?"

"I don't even know anymore," I say.

"Well, find out. What did you even go out there for, to look at the flowers?"

"We went for this," Vanessa says. She pulls out the Cloak

and shows it to her father.

His mouth drops open. "I-Is that what I think it is?" he asks.

"Yes. It's the Cloak. We risked our lives for this. Zim's grandmother is sick with Avian Scarring, and he wants to heal her. He was crazy enough to actually go for this, and he pulled it off."

"Well, *you* made the killing blow," I say.

"But you set me up for the shot." We continue to argue about who saved the day until...

"Ahem? Well that's great and all, but I don't remember teaching you to disobey and put your life on the line. I can't lose you like your mother!"

The room goes silent.

"That's the problem," Vanessa says. "You make us live our whole lives afraid. And you are the one who disappears her. You want to forget about her. Don't you want to make her memories live as long as possible? Why don't you tell me about her? Why did I have to learn about her... from a *dragon?*"

Vanessa's dad hangs his head and wipes his hand across his face.

"I want to be free," Vanessa continues. "Let me grow as a person and don't coddle me. I just want to adventure for new and exciting places—live life! We don't always have to stay here. We can move somewhere else or move into town or find a different place to have an alliance." Vanessa stops for a moment to breathe while her dad sits there, not even looking at her.

"But if you just want me to hide here forever and not care about anyone or anything outside this oasis, then take this, because I won't need it." She hands him the Life Limit. He holds it in his hands and turns the blade over and back.

"You truly are your mother's daughter," he says. "As much as I've tried to fight it, you're growing. Changing." He hands the sword back to her. "You keep this. You earned it."

Vanessa smiles—it's the happiest I've seen her in all the

time I've known her.

"And you," he says to me. I wince, thinking he's going to blame me again, but instead, he puts his hand on my shoulder. "You have earned that Cloak. Now don't you have someone to go save?"

"I do," I say. I look at Vanessa, and I don't even need to say anything. She knows I'll be back.

"Go!" she says. And I sprint out of the tent, take a running leap, and fly off, as fast as I can.

THE LETTER

Finally, I see my town below. Not wanting to be bombarded with questions about my whereabouts and wings, I land on the outskirts and proceed on foot. As I run through the town slipping and dodging through the streets, people whisper to each other, probably wondering where I was. It doesn't really matter now that I'm here. I'll just tell them when I'm done.

I run through the door of my house and go up to Grandma's room.

"Grandma, I did it, you're not gonna…"

I look at her bed, only to see an envelope.

I open it with shaking hands and read the letter inside, page for page.

When I am done, I am left in a daze.

Hello, Zim.

If you are reading this, you have completed your journey. Congratulations! Now I would celebrate with you, but I'm dead. (I'm sorry to be so blunt, but you know how I am.) Zim, please don't blame yourself for what had nothing to do with you. I suffered my wounds long before your time.

I am proud of you. You have grown into a fine young man, and I am happy to say that I raised you. The only way you are alive is because you have awakened your angel powers—by saving someone else. (If you somehow came here without unlocking your powers then you're lying because there is no way for you to have done it with your scrawny body. See, even dead ladies can keep it real.)

And now I'll tell you something you never knew: I myself was an angel. And so, in fact, was your mother. I was a soldier, too, of the Thirty-Sixth Battalion of the Holy Regiment. I was a young junior officer in recon who was eager to fight, but that's what got me here. I was stabbed by a Life Limit after I went too deep into enemy territory. I barely made it out alive, and then I knew my life was a ticking clock, so I resolved to make the most of every minute of it.

I retired, then had your mom, and now we have you, the Hero. I know that if your mother and father were here they'd be crying tears of joy to see that their baby has found who he truly is. (I obviously wouldn't cry. Crying is for softies!) But still, I am proud of you. And I hope you find happiness, in your very own way.

Love, Grandma

I look at the letter, reflecting on Grandma's last words. She was a strong, funny, different kind of woman. I guess I come from some strong, funny, different kind of stuff.

I look around this house. The house I grew up in. The last time I was here I didn't know how to fight a giant, let alone a dragon. I didn't have a friend like Vanessa. I feel a tear rolling down my cheek, and it drops onto the page. I turn the page to see Grandma's handwriting. "I told you—crying is for softies!" with a smiley face below. *That old lady sure had some jokes.*

As I wipe the tears away I get up and walk outside and inhale the fresh air. I start running towards the setting sun and open my wings. I soar high in the air, higher than an eagle. I feel all my angels with me. I fly into the clouds, wondering what will happen next.

ACKNOWLEDGMENTS

This book would not be possible without the hard work and dedication of the young people who, throughout one of the hardest collective years in our history, were committed to the dream of this book. We are grateful for their vision and for their vibrant imagination.

Special thanks to the leadership at Beacon House, including Kevin Hinton and Katherine Wiley, who with patience and flexibility worked with us in order to adapt our vision for the virtual world. We are grateful for their ongoing partnership and program support. And we offer special gratitude in memoriam to Derrick Roy, whose tragic loss during the course of this project we mourn. His excitement about this project motivated our authors to keep going. May these stories celebrate his memory.

We always feel gratitude for our dedicated team at Shout Mouse Press, and never more so than during this challenging year. We could not fully enact the mission of this project without the hard work of our Story Coaches: Bomani Armah, Drew Anderson, and Alexa Patrick, who met weekly to support each author as they wrote their stories. We are grateful for their commitment to centering youth voices and problem-solving through a year of unexpected challenges. We thank illustrator Tony White for his tremendous art, and for meeting individually with each author to capture the essence of their characters and universes. Thank you for bringing their stories to life! And to those working behind the scenes: editor Kathy Crutcher thoughtfully revised, structured, and combined these stories in a way that honors the young people and their mission; photographer Lana Wong gave our authors star treatment as she took their headshots; and designer Gigi Mascarenas ensured that our writers' work is presented professionally and with great attention and care.

Finally, we are grateful for the generous financial support from both individuals and institutions that make our work possible. This book was supported by project grants from The Max and Victoria Dreyfus Foundation, The Poetry Foundation, and The Sylarn Foundation. We appreciate your investment in our work, and most importantly, in the young people whose voices sing from these pages.

ABOUT THE AUTHORS

My name is Khalil Barnes and I was 14 years old when I wrote "Survivor." I like to read and also play video games. I live in Washington, DC and go to Washington Leadership Academy Public Charter School. I'm interested in learning to cook for myself and reading harder books. When I grow up, I would like to be a voice actor. People should read my story because it has an important message. "Stop bullying, and remember that everyone's life matters."

My name is Chase Cooper and I was 13 years old when I wrote "Hoops and Hopes." I live in Washington, DC and go to DC Prep. In my free time, I like to play basketball. I also really enjoy riding my bike, playing video games, and writing, although I am still getting used to doing it on a computer. (I have very nice handwriting.) When I grow up, I would like to be a civil engineer. People should read my story because I believe that during these times people should read more about young Black men. Also I believe that my story contains messages that are amusing, powerful, and useful.

My name is Kevin Crawford and I wrote "The Tale of Two Kobes" when I was a freshman at the Washington Leadership Academy. In my free time, I like to watch basketball, read, and nap. I enjoyed participating in this project because I was able to experience what it was like to be an author. I want my audience to know that if they experience a loss, their idols can still be remembered in their accomplishments. When I am older I want to go to college and become a math teacher.

My name is Josiah Ouabo and I was 13 years old when I wrote "Zim and the Quest for the Cloak." I live in Washington, DC and go to DC Prep. I like to have discussions with friends and also play video games. I'm interested in anime and documentaries. When I grow up I would like to be a United States Marine. People should read my story because it's fantasy and it is very suspenseful.

ABOUT THE ILLUSTRATOR

Tony White is an illustrator and animator. He recently graduated from VCUarts' Kinetic Imaging program. He hopes to work in the comic industry or on a serialized television program. You can find more of Tony's work in the Shout Mouse Press books *Game of Pharaohs* (2019) and *Breonna Marches Through Time* (2020).

ABOUT BEACON HOUSE

Beacon House is a nonprofit organization that provides afterschool education and youth development programs to children and families in Northeast Washington, DC. Its mission is to provide children in the greater Edgewood community of Washington, DC's Ward 5 with a safe, nurturing, life-expanding community in which to increase their academic achievement, discover their talents, and to grow into healthy adults who achieve their greatest potential. Beacon House's programs focus on closing the education achievement gap, and thus improving the economic trajectories of children in Ward 5 for whom generational poverty is most persistent.

Beacon House was founded in 1991 by Rev. Donald E. Robinson in response to an overwhelming need for education programs for youth in Edgewood. Today, according to a parent, Beacon House is "part of the glue that holds Edgewood together." Beacon House has been recognized as "One of the Best" nonprofits in Washington, DC by the Catalogue of Philanthropy since 2003, and its students and programs have been highlighted in recent years by national afterschool organizations including the Afterschool Alliance, National AfterSchool Association and the 50 State Afterschool Network.

beaconhouse
Where Learning Has A Home

ABOUT SHOUT MOUSE PRESS

Shout Mouse Press is a 501(c)3 nonprofit organization dedicated to centering and amplifying the voices of marginalized youth (ages 12+) via writing workshops, publication, and public speaking opportunities. The young people we coach are underrepresented—as characters and as creators—within young people's literature, and their perspectives underheard. Our work provides a platform for them to tell their own stories and, as published authors, to act as leaders and agents of change.

In collaboration with community-based partners, we have produced 45 books by 350+ youth who are incarcerated or formerly incacerated, Black, low-income, Latinx, Muslim, immigrants, from other marginalized communities and all the intersections therein from Greater Washington, DC. These authors change and reclaim the narrative, adding necessary complexity, empathy, and humanity to the stories of marginalized communities—and prove themselves as powerful thought leaders for all. There are currently over 90,000 Shout Mouse books in circulation across the country and around the world.

OTHER YOUNG ADULT TITLES FROM SHOUT MOUSE PRESS

How to Grow Up Like Me, Ballou Story Project (2014)

Trinitoga: Stories of Life in a Roughed-Up, Tough-Love, No-Good Hood, Beacon House (2014)

Our Lives Matter, Ballou Story Project (2015)

The Untold Story of the Real Me: Young Voices from Prison, Free Minds Book Club & Writing Workshop (2016)

Humans of Ballou, Ballou Story Project (2016)

The Day Tajon Got Shot, Beacon House (2017)

Voces Sin Fronteras: Our Stories, Our Truths, Latin American Youth Center (2018)

I Am the Night Sky: ... & other reflections by Muslim American youth, Next Wave Muslim Initiative (2019)

The Ballou We Know, Ballou Story Project (2019)

They Called Me 299-359, Free Minds Book Club & Writing Workshop (2020)

When You Hear Me (You Hear Us), Free Minds Book Club & Writing Workshop (2021)

For the full catalog of Shout Mouse books, including illustrated children's books, visit shoutmousepress.org.

For bulk orders, educator inquiries, and nonprofit discounts, contact orders@shoutmousepress.org.

Books are also available through Amazon.com, select bookstores, and select distributors, including Ingram, Baker & Taylor, and Follett.

CPSIA information can be obtained
at www.ICGtesting.com
Printed in the USA
BVHW021651090322
631062BV00011B/77